SHIBASHI QIGONG.

Fountain of Wellness

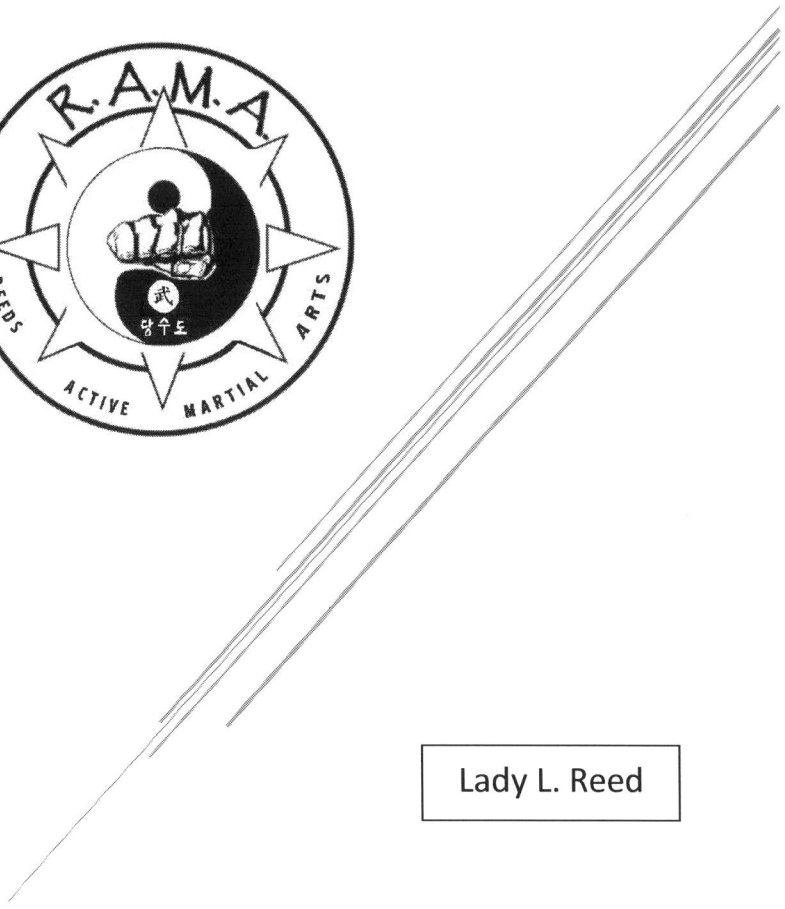

Lady L. Reed

Copyright 2020 Lady L. Reed

First printing: 2020

Printed in the United States of America

Publisher: RAMA & Wellness Club LLC

Contents

INTRODUCTION

This book is made to show you how to learn Shibashi Qigong. Most of the inner work is up to you. Please note that one can only feel their own energy if they learn to be sensitive about their own beingness.

Learning how to do Qigong is something beneficial because it can only help prevent stagnation or blockages. Life is about movement and energy.

My Story

Life is full of challenges. Sometimes, you will find yourself runover by heavy ones one after the other. I really felt so bad psychologically and physically after my first daughter was taken away from me by her father. That was a long traumatic story by itself that I would express in a different book. And yes, that was just one of those sad stories I had to go through this lifetime.

The reason I mentioned it though, is because I was going through that dilemma when I met my mentor Divina Martens in Hamburg, Germany. She introduced me into the world of Tai Chi, Qigong and Meditation in 1998. That was the time when I started practicing it with her and on my own. It helped me be centered, pull my Chi together, and work on other aspects of my life.

I was introduced to martial arts by my grandmother when I was 8 years old. She took me to a local tournament and showed me how people would fight in karate. I knew then that I did not want to be beaten up. At 16 though, I chose to do Taekwondo at the De LaSalle University as an extra-curriculum. Somehow, I kept finding myself pulled to all sorts of martial arts since then.

Anything physical that would make me feel alive and well was a big interest for me. I studied and searched for the right therapeutic methods. I also enjoy reading about health and wellness.

It was the beginning of my healing process.

If you would search the internet for Shibashi Qigong, you will find some materials on a PDF file. You will not find a lot though on how to do them step by step.

You could find some videos from some experts and amateurs, but none would slowly show you how it is done.

This is the only book on Shibashi Qigong that I know that will show you how to do it by reading and using this as a manual. It has links at the end of this book for you to watch videos on how to do each movement and barcodes for each said movements.

You can use the barcode by simply downloading a free barcode reader like QrScanner from the Play Store on your cellphone or your computer. It will then lead you to the YouTube Channel of Reed's Active Martial Arts and Wellness Club.

(Scan the barcode for the Video of Shibashi Movement #1-#18 to watch how the movements should look like or use the Video Links at the end of this book.)

"The teacher who is indeed wise does not bid you to enter the house of his wisdom but rather lead you to the threshold of your mind." – Kahlil Gibran

气 功

CHI FUNDAMENTALS

With the help of the internet, most people know by now what Chi is. If you google it, its definition from vocabulary.com would say: "the circulating life energy that in Chinese philosophy is thought to be inherent in all things."

(Chi or Qi in Chinese, Ki in Japanese, Prana in Hindu, Mana in Hawaiian)

Some literatures states that there are different kinds of Chi. They are mainly pertaining to inner chi and outward chi.

There are some videos on YouTube, where some so-called Qigong Master would demonstrate their Chi. Those were mostly people who trains to develop an iron shirt, wherein they believe that their chi would be strong enough that their body will not feel any pain.

So far, there is no reliable proof that one can manipulate the Chi to direct it to a person to harm them.

It has been written that in Traditional Chinese Medicine, they believe our body has meridians wherein the chi flows. In the meridian, there are hundreds of points that they believe to either harm or heal you. It was also written on books that those meridians corresponds to the main organs like, kidney, bladder, gall bladder, liver, stomach, spleen, small intestines, large intestines, heart, lungs, triple warmer, pericardium, conception vessel and governing vessel. It is the backbone of acupressure and acupuncture.

You can feel your own Chi by placing both of palms infront of each other, imagine the ball of energy between them and feel it expanding as you breathe in. For some, it may feel like a tingling sensation or like a magnet poles opposing each other.

You can try to feel the energy of your surroundings by using you palms to and letting the chi move it as you empty your mind.

YIN AND YANG PRINCIPLE

Yin as many already are informed, pertains to the female qualities and Yang is to male qualities. In traditional Chinese medicine, there is a whole study that explains which body part corresponds to its kind. It is more than just the opposites as the general mass of people heard about.

Everyone has Yin and Yang. Balancing it in within the body makes the chi can flow freely.

There is a deficit and overflow of both that some TCM doctors consider to be symptomatic to the diseases or conditions that people get. They also have the necessary herbal knowledge to treat such Yin and Yang imbalances.

One of the ways to balance it though is practicing Qigong every day.

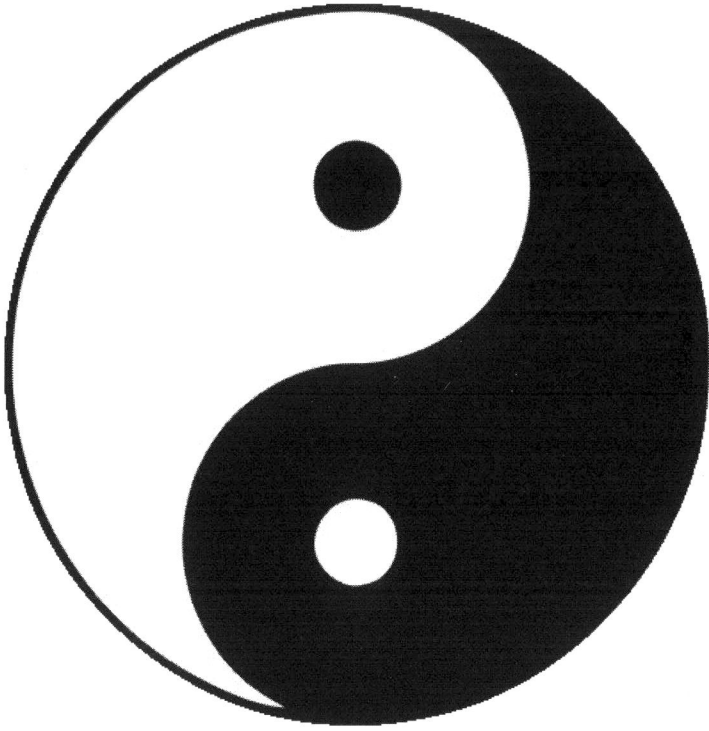

WHAT IS QIGONG?

Qigong is a set of exercises developed by the shaolin monks in China. It is translated to energy work. It helps your energy to flow back to a state of wellness.

The word Qi is the same as Chi or Prana which means life energy. It is believed in traditional Chinese medicine that our body has meridians with certain points where the life energy flows. If it is blocked, they believe that it can cause diseases.

The word Gong is Chinese for cultivation, skill, or exercise. Together, Qigong is translated to breathing exercise or cultivation of your life energy.

Qigong is moving the body in slow movements stationary while breathing. It is an internal work which they also call Nehgong.

Everybody is born with life energy in them. It is up to the person how he/she would be aware and would know how to harness its power.

Some Qigong exercises are done standing, seated or supine position. Each movement is typically done repetitively with your breath.

It is recognized as Mind-Body Medicine in China. Through cultivating the Chi through Qigong, the imbalances in the energy flow in the body can be balanced and therefore bring about wellness, and in some cases, even heal a chronic illness.

Qigong is also known as a movement and breathing meditation. Some of its movements can be seen in Tai Chi which is a slow-moving exercise or walking meditation that was practiced by the shaolin monks for thousands of years.

There are three main kind of Qigong. 1. Qigong for martial arts. 2. Qigong for medical healing. 3. Qigong for spiritual advancement.

You must be familiar with some Qigong forms already like Tai Chi, Baduanjin, Yi Jin Jing, and Bagua.

Like some martial arts, Tai Chi for example has also different styles like Chen Style, Yang Style, Wu Style, Hao Style and Sun Style.

It is not necessary the style that makes a Qigong practice better, but it is the knowledge and experience of it that makes it so.

Its importance is in ability of becoming one with nature as a human being. Like in Taoism (Daoism), your goal for this lifetime is to achieve balance in all areas of life. When there is balance, harmony can exist.

There is a whole science behind Qigong in China and there is a lot more of information if you really want to dig deeper in it.

WHAT IS SHIBASHI?

Shibashi is a Chinese word for 18 movements, therefore making it a set of 18 Qigong movements that is done stationary and repetitively.

It is a Chinese mandarin word. Shi means 10, Ba means 8, shi also means movement.

It has been scientifically tested in preventing diseases and promoting health and wellness by professors and medical physicians in Europe, China, as well as America.

HISTORY

In ancient time in China, the Taoists monks were known to combine martial arts practices with breathing exercises, with the intent of enhancing strength, and even to acquire magical powers. They also believe that the mountains and mostly nature is a great source of spiritual power.

The Shaolin monks practiced Sanchin form. They added the martial arts applications to it. Adopted from yoga, the Sanchin's breathing were to stimulate the energies of body and mind.

It was around the beginning of the first century B.C. that the Indian Buddhist monks migrated from India to China.

They spread the teachings of Buddhism and Indian philosophy to China, which became the source of meditation and martial arts.

Bodhidharma (c. 520 A.D.), was among the first monk who traveled to China and taught the teachings of Qigong, Meditation and Martial Arts.

Qigong is a spiritual practice for thousands of years until the China's Communist period under Mao Tung. He banned its practices for 30 years.

A Qigong Master, scientist and healer developed Shibashi based on Tai Chi & Qigong with some movements of Yang Style around 1970s. He also adopted the Wu Style stance wherein the legs are as wide as the shoulders.

The Qigong Masters found a way around the banning of the religious practices. That was when Professor Lin made sure that it is only for health purposes.

The traditional Chinese medicine included Tai Chi and Qigong as one of its foundational exercises in promoting mental and physical health and wellness.

It is still practiced by many martial artists, though few can truly harness its power.

BENEFITS

Practicing Shibashi Qigong can have lots of benefits if done daily. Try it out yourself and find out if you would really feel the difference in your state of mind and body.

These are the benefits that one may get by practicing Qigong:

Doing Qigong, like Tai Chi, Baduanjin and Shibashi is proven to relieves stress.

Your nerves are going to be calm through the movements and breathing.

Qigong improves circulation of blood.

It also improves your breathing i.e. flow of oxygen to the organs.

It keeps the Chi flowing.

Your concentration will improve.

The movements help treat Parkinson. Some even says it helps prevent dementia.

Like having a massage, improves the quality of your sleep.

Because it is considered a meditation, you will get rid of anxiety.

It can help reduces pain of fibromyalgia and arthritis.

It helps lower high blood pressure.

Since the movements builds up your muscle, any muscular and skeletal problem may be prevented. It makes your joints and muscles strong.

It may improve your balance.

It stops depression.

It can also improve your posture.

It may improve mobility.

It can keep one young.

When you practice daily, you will notice an increase in your mental clarity.

Your digestion may improve.

Yours conditions related to the nervous system may also improve.

Since it is also an inner work, your spiritual energy is bound to increase.

POINTERS

The number one thing that you should do before you start practicing is to relax.

Relax every part of your body. Wear loose clothing.

Try to empty your mind. There should be a list of things to do in your mind while you are doing Qigong. This session is designed for you to spend time with yourself in the present moment.

In practicing Shibashi Qigong, you may do it outdoors or indoors. A peaceful environment with good air circulation preferably, not to be done where there's fire or heavy thunderstorm outside.

Perform the movements as slow as possible for you. Nobody is going to judge how you move. Do not worry so much about not being coordinated. It will all improve with time. Every movement must be comfortable for you.

When breathing, use your diaphragm. Breathe in through your nose and breathe out through your mouth. Contract your abdomen when you are breathing out. Breath in deeply and let your lungs be filled in its capacity.

Make sure your legs are square to your shoulders. Imagine a string tied to the top of your head pulling you up, making your back straight and your chin not pointing out. Tilt your pelvis slightly in. Place your tongue on your upper palate. Do not be rigid on the position.

If you practice it daily for at least three months, you would be able to see and feel its benefits.

Qigong is a lifelong art. You learn in your own phase and will continue learning more in due time. Mastery on it comes only through the practice.

"The breath is the essence of all religion. Cure of all illness." – Rumi

"Get more Spirit through breathing." – John-Roger

SHIBASHI MOVEMENTS

Shibashi has eighteen movements. Like in yoga, each movement has a name and can be done repetitively and by itself.

1. Waving your hands to the sea.

Breathe in as you raise your arms while you bend your knees slightly, together slowly. Breathe out as you lower your arms while you straighten your legs back slowly.

I would suggest to repeat the movement at least 8 times. You can do the movements as often as you want.

Your legs will be stronger and your shoulders.

2. Opening Chest

Lift your arms at the front as you breathe in slowly, then open your arms slowly to the side while bending the knees down.

Breathe slowly out as you bring the arms back to the front and down to your side while standing up.

3. Painting a Rainbow

Breathe in as you hold your arms above your head as you bend to the left. Then breathe out as you keep your arms above your head as you bend to the right.

It is a kind of bending sideward wherein you would feel the stretch on your ribcage. Imagine holding a big ball when you bend to the sides.

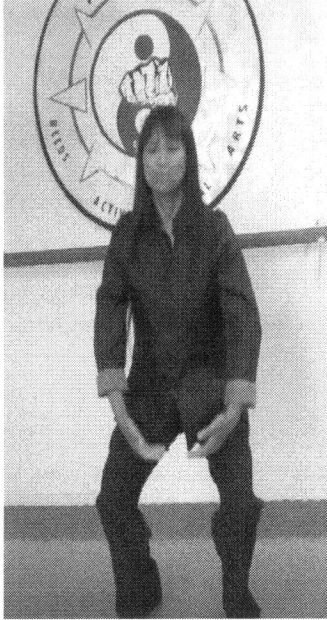

4. Separating Clouds

Bend your knees and scoop the cloud as you breathe in.

Breathe out as you straighten your legs and move your hands away from each other like you are separating the cloud.

5.   Pulling   the   Silk
Thread

Like pulling an arrow from the bow, extend your left arm out front as you breathe in and pull the invisible string out to your back as you turn your head back while bending your knees.

Breathe out and let go of the thread as you straighten your back leg.

6. Rowing the Boat

Breathe in as you bring your palms up on your side to the level of your shoulders.

Breathe out as you circle your arms downward, bending from your hip while keeping your back straight.

If you do this slowly, you will feel the stretch on your hamstring and lower back.

7. Balancing the Ball

With the left palm facing down on the side of your waist, the right hand holding a ball with palms facing up diagonally to the left side while you bend your knees, you breathe in.

Breathe out as you do the same motion to your right side with the left hand holding the ball, left palm up and the right palm next to right side of your waist.

8. Praising   the
Moon

Bring your palms at the front like carrying a baby, bend your knees as you breathe in and turn your spine to the back as you lift both of your arms carrying an invisible baby into straight legs.

Breathe out swinging to the right side doing the same motion.

The twisting of the spine keeps your vertebrae flexible.

9. Pushing Hands

With left palm facing down on your left waist, bend your knees as you breathe in and push your right palm infront of you.

Breathe out as you do the same motion with the left hand.

10. Playing with Clouds

Breathe in slowly as you lift your right palm infront of your chest, bend your knees and look at your palm as you move your upper body to your right.

Breathe out slowly as you lift your left palm infront of your chest, keep your knees bent and look at your palm as you move your upper body to your left.

11. Scooping Water from the Sea and Bathing with it

Put your left leg out, with toes pointing up, lean forward from your hips, scoop some water from the sea motion as you breathe in.

As you breathe out, lift your arms to your chest then open your arms as you lean back.

Balance is the key here and stretching your pecs.

12. Rolling Waves

Bring your hands to your waist level with palms downward as you step with your left leg 45 degree with your heel, breathe in.

As you breathe out, push an your hands out extending arms with your weight going into the front foot.

This movement can be used in a self-defense movement.

13. Spreading the Bird's Wings

The movement is like scooping water from the sea but it is done in front of you with the left leg in front, shifting your weight to the front foot as you breathe in, move the arms together.

Breathe out as you spread your arms out, shifting your weight to the back leg and breathing out fast.

14. Dragon's Breath

Breathe in bending your knees as you bring your fist to your side, punch out with your left as you breathe out, circle your wrist bringing the fist back to your side.

Breathe in as you punch out with right, circle your wrist bringing the fist back.

Stay in the squat position until you finish these movements.

15. Flying Goose

From standing position, breathe in in as you bend your knees, bringing the hands cross to the front.

Breathe out as you stand back up and lift up the arms on your side to shoulder level.

16. Windmill

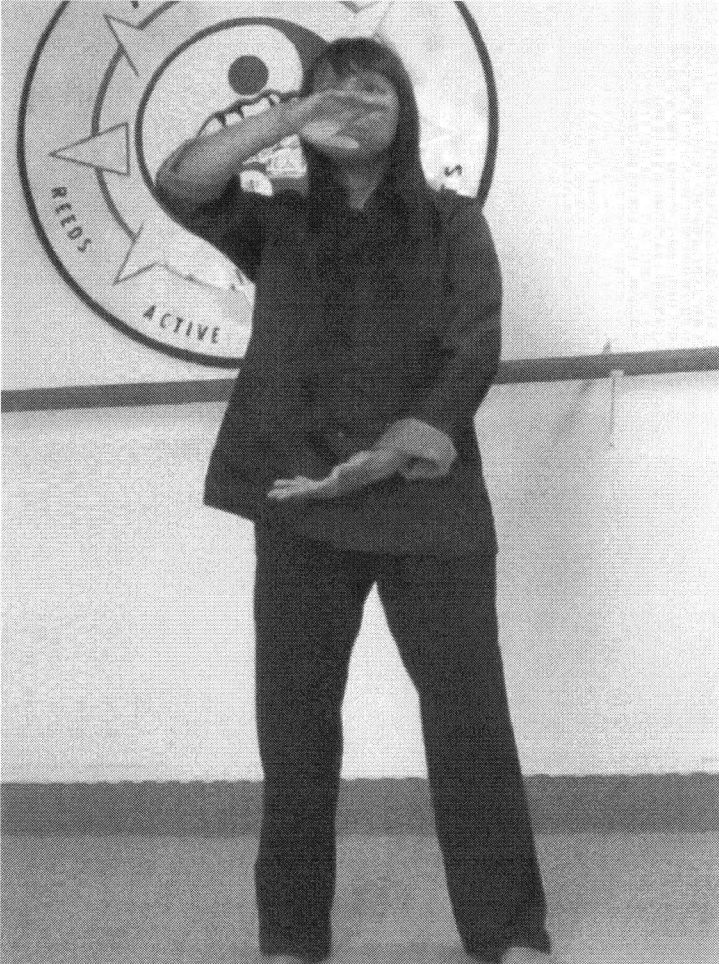

From standing position, imagine holding a big ball infront of you. Turn the ball as you bring the ball to your left side, breathing in. Breathe out as you lean forward bring the ball down.

Breathe in as you turn the ball to your right side, then turn the ball as you bring it high infront of you. Turn the ball as you bring it to your left side again.

It is actually a long breath in and short breath out.

17. Bouncing Ball

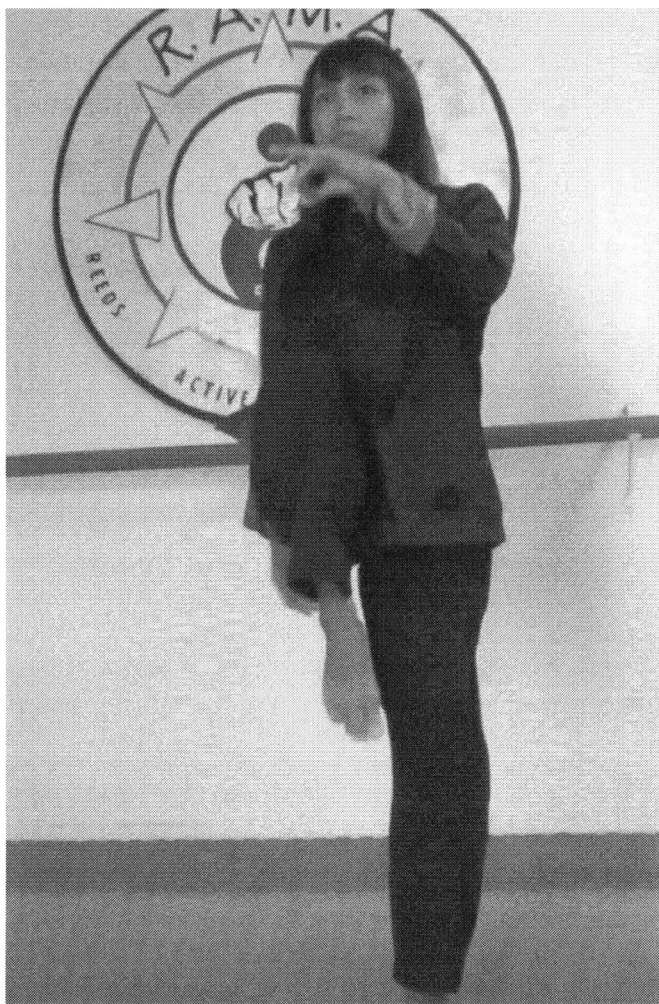

Imagine a thread connected to your knee and as you pull the thread up, you hop up a little, breathe in.

Breathe out as you let go of the thread and the knee.

Do the movement with alternating legs.

The short breaths will free your nostrils.

18. Closing

Circle out your arms bringing it on top of your head as you breathe in. Breathe out as you push down your hands.

This closing movement can be done with closed eyes and visualizing a ball of light on top of the head when the arms are on top.

Then push down the ball of light infront of you like a magnetic light pulling away any pain or negativity from your body into the ground.

Traditional Bow

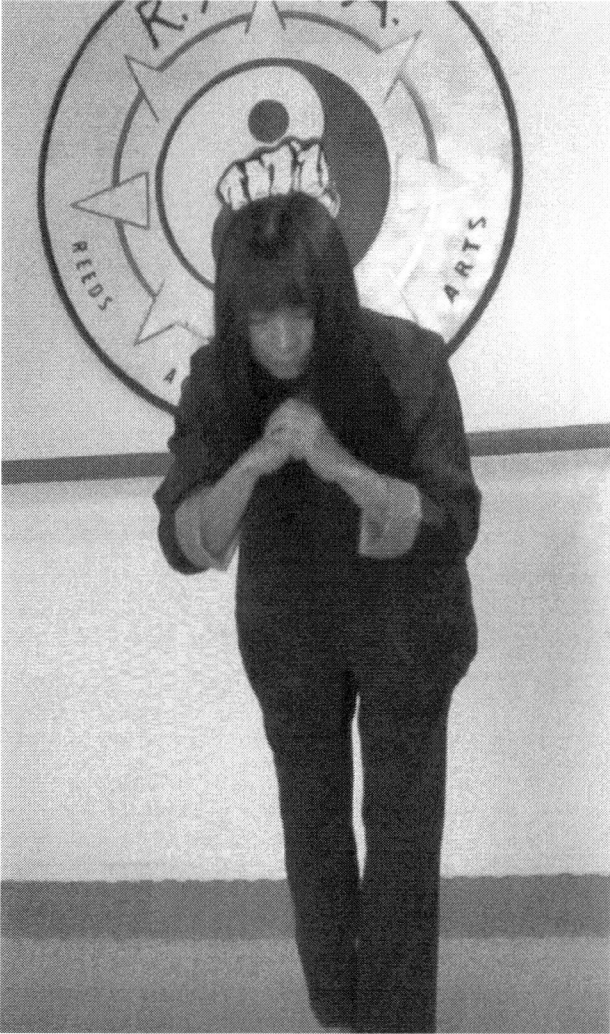

A Chinese traditional bow is bringing your hands together with the right fist being covered by the left hand. Simply bow with it as a sign of respect.

To understand how chi works, you do not need to believe anything. It becomes only clear to open-minded people.

Religion is not needed to welcome its presence in our physical body and mind.

The simple explanation of it as a form of energy that is attached to physical body running in meridians should be enough to grasp its presence. Everyone has it.

"He who conquers himself is the mightiest warrior." - Confucius

MEDITATION

Since Qigong is also considered a breathing meditation, always try to find a place for it to avoid disturbance. When you meditate, you gather energy from your environment as well as from the inside going out. It will make a lot of sense if you have a clean place or corner that is only for meditation.

If you could meditate at the same time daily, your body will develop the habit of doing it. After some time, your physical body will automatically do it.

Relax and let yourself come into stillness. Let your breath be on with your movement and simply watch it. There is no reason to force both your breathing and movement.

If you find yourself thinking about what you are going to do or what you have done, see it and let it go. Bring your awareness between your eyebrows and come back to witnessing your breath and flow with the movement.

Like most things, it takes time to remember the sequence of the 18 movements. Take it easy on yourself. If you can do at least a couple of the movements and remember doing it daily, then it will be easy to learn the rest.

There is no right or wrong in meditating when your intention is to go inside and let go of this world's illusion.

NOTES:

_____

_____

_____

_____

_____

_____

_____

_____

_____

_____

_____

_____

_____

_____

_____

_____

_____

_____

_____

_____

_____

_____

_____

_____

_____

_____

_____

_____

CHINESE WORDS

Dantian – a region 3 centimeters below the navel

Xinghai – a point between the eyebrows

Yin – female polarity

Yang – male polarity

Dao – way, method

Xing – behavior, conduct

Shen – God, Spirit

Hetu – River Map

Bagua – eight trigrams

Neiyao – internal medicine

Waiyao – external medicine

Xianglong – dragon

Fuhu – tiger

Taichi – supreme ultimate

Wuji – supreme void

Jing – stillness

Chan – meditation

ACKNOWLEGEMENT

My gratitude goes in fortitude to my husband and Grandmaster David L. Reed, who watched and helped me grow in the world of martial arts. I am also thankful to my mentor Divina Martens, who taught and helped me decades ago to control my emotions and cultivate my chi.

They both believed in my potentiality and capabilities that I can only perform, doing my best.

I want to acknowledge the presence of my children in my life too, because living would be less fun without them.

Thanks to Grandmaster Eric Lee for giving me the opportunity to learn and advance more in my life.

Thanks to Grandmaster Leo Fong (92 yrs. Old) for inspiring me to continue my qigong practice with his Chi Fung, and to Soke GM "Big Cat" Frederick Peterson (95 yrs. Old) for simply showing that to live as long as they do, one has to stay active physically, mentally and having a strong faith in God.

Thanks to my Sifu Dr. Z for his knowledge of Daoism and TCM.

I'm also grateful to Kyosa James Behtash for giving me the idea of having a barcode that links to a video that demonstrate the readers/students how the movement is being done.

A special thanks to Kyosa Skee Goedhart for creating the logo video of R.A.M.A. that I used for making the video that KJN Reed took.

Thanks to a handful of real friends and students whom I know will always be there in this lifetime.

I am also in gratitude of my MSIA spiritual family and to God, who is my main source.

VIDEO LINK:

1. Waving Hands at the Sea
   https://youtu.be/F-bFzmQZa_4

2. Opening Chest
   https://youtu.be/fCiDoAZo8HQ

3. Painting a Rainbow
   https://youtu.be/D2cVDKkIGTA

4. Separating Clouds
   https://youtu.be/wKU7MUXVzHY

5. Pulling the Silk Thread
   https://youtu.be/q59ATRjqpUM

6. Rowing the Boat
   https://youtu.be/1pAJvSbRBr0

7. Balancing the Ball
   https://youtu.be/-cUV0R2ViEQ

8. Praising the Moon
   https://youtu.be/45xPVQFPtWU

9. Pushing Hands

   https://youtu.be/QT19NUPfYfk

10. Playing with Clouds

   https://youtu.be/aYZZnh4KZgE

11. Scooping Water from the Sea

   https://youtu.be/YyHQHJLHMng

12. Rolling Waves

   https://youtu.be/1m9yXpUqOFc

13. Spreading the Birds Wings

   https://youtu.be/TwedLs9Vq_s

14. Dragon's Breath

   https://youtu.be/W1Pjsa5bY9w

15. Flying Goose

   https://youtu.be/Ix2ET2Thco0

16. Windmill

   https://youtu.be/Nnf3AmImIWc

17. Bouncing Ball

   https://youtu.be/dZXA_WTFcow

18. Closing

https://youtu.be/Kr8bq_Wj3Xs

Prevention is the best medicine.

Have a peaceful heart, a good body, an active mind, and balanced personality.

SUGGESTED READING MATERIALS

It is advisable to broaden your knowledge about certain topics to support what you believe in. Here are some books I would suggest for you to read:

The Essential Guide to Energy Healing by Dr. Michael Andron and Ben Andron 2012

Qigong for Health and Martial Arts by Dr. Yang, Jwing-Ming 1985

Tai Chi for Health by Edward Maisel 1963

Essentials of Tai Chi and Qigong Course Guidebook by David Doria Ross

Tai Chi Classice by Waysun Lao 1977

Tai Chi Chuan An Ancient Chinese Way of Exercise eto Achieve Health & Tranquility by Sophia Delza 1973

Chinese Qigong Illustrated by Yu Gongbao 1995

The Way of Qigong by Cohen

ABOUT THE AUTHOR

Lady L. Reed was born in Manila, Philippines in 1974. Her martial arts practice started when she was 16 years old.

She is the co-founder of Reed's Active Martial Arts System in California, USA, that includes the health and wellness aspect of the martial arts styles as a whole through practicing the styles of Tang Soo Do, Taekwondo, Jeet Kune Do, Wei Kuen Do, Wing Chun, Escrima, Tai Chi Chuan, Shibashi Qigong, Baduanjin, and Yoga.

She was a martial arts hall of fame inductee 2016-2020, USA national champion martial arts master and actress.

Being certified in Shiatsu, Acupressure & Reflexology in 1993, she become a certified massage therapist in Los Angeles in 2015. Her modalities are Swedish massage, Deep Tissue Massage, Pregnancy & Infant Massage, Geriatric Massage, Trigger Point and Reiki Massage. She is a Reiki Master von Bryce Winston.

Her DVDs, namely are Dynamic Energy, Dynamic Stretching, Dynamic Massage, A girl from Copacobana from Warreners Entertainment and Emc Videos, and Qigong for Beginners from Peace Unleashed.

She is also the author of R.A.M.A. Student Handbook eBook and paperback, The Mind of a Champion Revealed eBook, Create Your Best in 5 Steps eBook & paperback and A Tender Heart Poetry Book eBook & paperback.

Printed in Great Britain
by Amazon